The Seasoning

Elaine Cannon

The SEASONING

Bookcraft
Salt Lake City, Utah

Library of Congress Catalog Card Number: 80-70857
ISBN 0-88494-420-4

First Printing, 1981

Lithographed in the United States of America
PUBLISHERS PRESS
Salt Lake City, Utah

To my friends
from whom I've learned

Contents

Introduction

George M. Trevelyan's *History of England* reports a speech recorded by the Venerable Bede, given in the seventh century by an Anglo-Saxon thegn in favor of his nation's accepting Christianity. It holds a special truth for me.

"The present life of man upon earth, O king, seems to me, in comparison with that time which is unknown to us, like to the swift flight of a sparrow through the house wherein you sit at supper in winter, with your Ealdormen and thegns, while the fire blazes in the midst and the hall is warmed, but the wintry storms of rain or snow are raging abroad. The sparrow, flying in at one door and immediately out at another, whilst he is within, is safe from the wintry tempest; but, after a short space of fair weather, he immediately vanishes out of your sight, passing from winter into winter again. So this life of man appears for a little while, but of what is to follow or what went before we know nothing at all."

Similarly each of us knows little, really, of the struggle the other makes in life, through our winters and through our summers, too. Our comings in and our goings out of the proverbial cold and sunshine help us become what, at last, we are going to be.

Such seasoning teaches that every problem has a gift in its hand, that there are precious blessings in adversities and trials in every success. Spring feels warmer, leafing is lovelier after living through the winter sparseness of life.

Someone has said that to feel tenderness after long numbness, to turn to scripture after a year in the marketplace or to health after a bout with relentless aging, to remember what once it seemed life could hold, is music after long silence, and it makes the soul flex its wings and, clumsy as any fledgling, try the air again.

So it is.

This is a book about soul-flexing, about the winter sparrow-times of life and the summer robin-times they herald. Part of the book was previously published under the title of *The Summer of My Content.*

Winter

"... I was glad of what I had, as a winter bird is, that will come into your hand for a little crumb, though in plenteous times she would but mock you from the topmost bough. I took my crumb, and behold! it was the Lord's Supper."

(Mary Webb, *Precious Bane*, Modern Library.)

Winter Comes
When the Heart Breaks

Winter comes in life not by solstice, not even by the first snowfall. Winter comes when the heart breaks, regardless of the season. And often the heart breaks because of what we do to each other.

It begins early in life when choosing up sides for a game. For example, nobody should be chosen last. Every time! When everybody else gets chosen for a side when you are playing teams in baseball and you join a side simply because you are the last one left, it is no good. It's terrible. Humiliation. Rejection. Heartbreak.

Winter.

And that's what happened to me for one whole school year.

It was the time of depression in the land. Girls wore hand-me-down dresses of cotton print—sash tied, puff sleeved, and hemmed to meet our cotton socks at the knees. Our sashes were forever being torn loose, and the socks seldom stayed put. Baseball was our life, and dresses were poor attire for it. But so it was.

Two baseball diamonds had been made in a lot adjoining the school—one for boys and one for girls. Whenever the ground was somewhat dry during the year, we played baseball at recess, baseball at lunch, and baseball after classes. It was because of Maude and Virginia. They loved baseball. They were sisters and the most incredibly good baseball players you could imagine. We all worshipped at their feet and declared them undisputed captains of the two teams.

Maude was older and could pitch "faster than sight." Why, half the hitters missed half her throws most of the time! She was smart as a mynah bird, and cagey. She had been sick a time back and had had to repeat a year of school, the way they did then, so this put the sisters in the same grade, two grades ahead of me.

Virginia was bigger. She could catch a fly without a mitt. She could bat that ball, then lope around home before the out team rallied to act past their shoutings. She threw the ball like a boy.

So their teams pretty well balanced, no matter how the rest of us got portioned out. Each time we played, the opening ceremony was repeated. We would choose up sides for teams, with Maude and Virginia "eagle-clawing" the bat to determine who got first choice and therefore who chose last.

After a while I realized there were never going to be any surprises in this for me. I was left until last every time. Out of all the regulars who raced to the playing field, I was always chosen last. Maybe it was an understood fact, but that didn't help my hurt. Our baseball game was one of those times in life when enthusiasm didn't make up for skill. After a while it wasn't who was chosen when that interested me, it was which of the sisters would have last choice, because that made all the difference to me.

If Maude eagle-clawed the bat, that meant she got first choice, and Virginia got me. Which was just fine, because she would pass off this crisis to her team with, "Oh, well, I can hit hard enough for both of us," and beckon me after her.

Somehow I was comforted by that inclusive statement.

If Virginia eagle-clawed the bat, Maude was left with me. And that's where the trauma came in. Virginia would choose her last team member and then, inevitably, Maude would turn and walk out to the playing field, as if I didn't exist. Not a sign! Not a beckon or an instruction! Not a comment or even a complaint! Nothing. As if I didn't exist.

Whenever things turned out this way, I would shiver, even if the fall's last warmth still hung over the school grounds. But I never threw up, which was some kind of personal victory, because a sensitive nine-year-old with a digestive system like mine could stand only so much social shivering.

There was a period when Virginia had a run of winnings at eagle claws, and I was about to give up baseball and be rid of the anguish of Maude's silent treatment of me. But one day I read something in the *Woman's Home Companion* while baby-sitting that gave me renewed hope. "Don't let your passions spoil your dreams," a youth writer counseled. I don't think it had anything to do with baseball, but baseball was my dream right then. My mortification over when I was chosen had to be kept under control if any dreams of making it on the diamond with the older girls were to come true.

So I kept on going to the field, but now I had primed myself for the test. Positive action was to replace negative reaction.

First, I parted my hair down the middle and abandoned my barrette. Though the effect with my long narrow face wasn't necessarily an improvement, it was a change. I hoped it would be an attention-getter. The outcome of that effort, however, did little for my situation. Nobody noticed.

Next, I studied my facial expressions—grimacing, smiling, squinting, and sweetening in front of the bathroom mirror. For hours. I concluded that a lift to my eyebrows would make me look more alive, more capable at play. Maybe then I'd be selected earlier in the lineup. I couldn't stand the tweezers, but I had seen one of the roomers at my friend's house use a straightedge to clean off her stray hair. So I took Dad's razor and stroked my brow. In one sweep the entire half of my left eyebrow disappeared, which wasn't what I had in mind. There was nothing to do but match the other side to it.

It never matched, of course, but I had to stop trying, or I'd be left without even a dot over my eye! I tried marking the eyebrows back into being by using a burnt match; but people kept wiping "soot" off my face, and I was left until last anyway.

Next I spread graham crackers with pink powdered sugar frosting, folded them in Wonder Bread wax wrappings, and hid them in my coat pockets to produce at eagle-claw time. Bribery didn't work either. They ate my cookies, those captains, while choosing up sides, leaving me until last. Every time.

Though the chill winds blew through me, I didn't give up. I took to praying on the spot, urgently crying out in my soul, "Please don't let me be last. Please let one of them choose me sooner." But if my prayers reached heaven, the signals weren't heard by Maude or Virginia.

Finally, I took to silently rooting that my "enemy" Maude would win at eagle claws so Virginia could choose last. Then I wouldn't have to suffer the humiliation of being ignored by Maude at the end of the choosing. This shifted my concern from me to something else clear through that season. That was good.

That's how I learned to face life's winter, a storm as it came, not a season in full, with "self" at the bottom of the list of concerns.

The traumas of childhood often mark the beginning of the stamina for certain suffering in maturity. I have always believed that there is a very grown-up spirit inside the infant body. The kind of thing that hurts in childhood can hurt in maturity. The ramifications may not be so sweeping, and understanding the self-control can modify, but the roots are the same.

Maybe that's how I understood about Gerrard and could comfort his folks some when the need arose.

When they found Gerrard dead "by his own hand" at sixteen, people exclaimed foolishly, "Why would he do such a thing? Why?"

Why, indeed. The answer is implicit in the question. That's exactly why Gerrard did a thing like that. Nobody knew enough about him deep inside to even arouse suspicions along the way. It was done and over, that tragedy, with people still wondering why.

Perhaps it was Gerrard's way of ditching the winter in his life. Winter, all day, every season, year after year. And heartbreak.

He was left until last at choosing time. Nobody rooted for him when they fenced at the church on activity night or wrestled at the gym. Nobody mopped the blood off his nose when the customary after-school fight finally stopped.

And nobody ever invited him to a birthday party.

Over the years Gerrard had grown fat and fluffy from fast foods stuffed in to while away the lonely hours. He ate lunch alone in the cafeteria, wandered solo through shopping malls on Saturdays, and had the top row to himself at all the games.

Maybe people tried.

Maybe Gerrard tried.

But it wasn't enough.

The problem seemed to be that Gerrard had never known about "caring." He was a foster child who had been taken in, hopefully at last, by a small-town childless older couple. They were unequipped for the abrasive patterns of personal insecurity from childhood hurts that Gerrard had developed. The foster parents gave him room and board, clothes and equipment, an allowance for treats and good times with his friends. But there were no friends. They didn't know how to help him with that. And they didn't know how to give of themselves.

Gerrard gave people nothing except the occasion for the question of "Why?" at his suicide.

Oh, why do we do what we do to each other?

Dachau, one of those infamous Nazi concentration camps of hell for Jews, has been turned into a kind of memorial to remind people what people have done to each other. There is a sign there that sobers the visitor: "Man cannot trust himself in the hands of men." The evidence seems obvious at Dachau.

I had read about concentration camps and had recoiled with my generation in disbelief at the hearings after World War II. Being there was deep agony for me. My mind, my heart, the very core of me, was overwhelmingly bruised by my personal Dachau experience.

I went curious, of course, but somewhat hesitant, too, and at the insistence of a dear friend who felt everyone should see this place so mankind would never forget. And I will never forget.

Doggedly we began the charted course through sparse exhibits and pitiful pictures of the devastation — of emaciated, tortured children of God. Hundreds and thousands of them, their souls staring out through cavernous eyes.

I couldn't really look at the pictures. It was much like people walk by a coffin at a viewing, only glancing toward the deceased unless they are halted by a family member who asks, "Doesn't she look lovely?" Then it is the more painful to look, and you wish you'd done it on your own.

Once at Dachau I looked at a picture closely at my companion's invitation. Life sprang from the flat photograph of people who had suffered even beyond desperation. My heart constricted with cold, deep and biting, like being chosen last as a child.

It was overwhelming to me. I somehow felt implicated.

("Forgive me," I silently prayed. "Oh, forgive me, Lord. I was growing up. I was way out in Utah when all of this happened. But forgive me for silence, for not understanding, for not caring enough for so long.")

We pressed forward through each phase of the complex in mounting horror — on through barnlike barracks with wall-to-wall, ceiling-to-floor bunks; on to community rest-room facilities;

on, then, to those sinister bathhouses where gas jetted through "shower heads" to kill the numberless masses; on finally, depressingly, incredibly out past open trenches like the ones where the dead had been dumped and plowed under.

Unprepared for the impact of this place, I wanted to cry out in a long overdue wail loud enough and long enough for the dead to hear—the killed and the killers to hear and know. For all mankind and God in his heaven to hear and to know.

But no cry came. The ache was too deep, the awful awareness of man's evil ability to hurt man was too constricting for anything but silence.

They say the sun never shines over Dachau, so dark were the deeds of those days. It is true my own tears fell unnoticed, so wet were the skies while we were there, and I thought of the old French saying, "Il pleut dans mon cœur comme il pleut sur la ville." (It rains in my heart as it rains in the city.)

One goes home to teach the children never to kill anything, even a fly. And never to break a heart.

What puts winter in one person's heart may pass as only a temperature drop in another's. Fear of the unknown, physical injury, some kind of deprivation, haven't contributed to my stormy times. People have and still can. People always have affected me deeply one way or the other, chilling or warming my sensitive soul either by their suffering or their joy, or mine.

Once I met a successful businessman who smiled slowly when our introductions were over.

"You don't remember me," he said.

"I'm sorry. No. Should I?" I regretted the oversight, however innocent.

"No problem. We were depression kids when our paths crossed before. I was poor folks from the shack at the top of the long wooden steps where the hill slopes into town. Remember the place?"

I remembered.

"I lived there all during my high school years and didn't have a friend in the world. No one would even dance with me. One winter's night at a church function I mustered my nerve to ask you to dance. I knew I was in over my head, your being one of the 'in' crowd and all, but I decided to go for broke."

"What happened?" I ventured.

"We danced! Not only that, but you were nice to me. Maybe this sounds crazy, but it's true. That day hope came back into my life. How could I ever forget you?"

("Oh, forgive us, Lord, for man's inhumanity to man in all the small ways, too!")

Winter comes not by the solstice but when the heart breaks. When our tranquility is threatened, our loved one lost, our dream dashed, our regrets engulfing, and whatever else, a pall comes upon us. It is only endurable finally, when Christ becomes part of our being. If we did to others as he did, the tide of error in man's relationships with man would soon be stemmed. Christ is our model. He asked forgiveness for those who crucified him. He gave the sop of friendship to his betrayer and took the basin to wash the dust and pride from the feet of his servants and disciples. He spoke of casting the first stone, of beams and motes, and of how to treat prodigals. He blessed the unclean and comforted the mourner. He defended Mary before the bustling efficiency of Martha. He labeled loving others as the great commandment and warned that because of iniquity the love of many would "wax cold."

To keep our own love from waxing cold, we can strive to be more like him. We can be a light and not a judge, caring about others enough to save reputations, protecting the innocent, sparing heartbreak by what we do or do not to each other.

It is indeed a wintry day when we live as if Jesus had never lived, as if he had never died, as if we had never once been touched by him and his spirit of love.

Christmas
and Hospitals

W inter—the season with its own systems of shutting out and shutting in, of heart chills and frostbite—brings Christmas as its bonus package. Christmas is a kind of putting by against the season of shivers, slush, sickness, and sadness. We come home again, then, in an annual ritual of healing, when the age-old benedictions of friendship and family ties give us peace from our problems, warmth after our cold, security from the strange storms that beset us.

I love every pagan, Christian, commercial, sentimental, under-planned, overdone aspect of it.

I love the legends and the myths as well as the tender truth of its beginning as recorded in sacred writ.

Christmas always has been a sweet and hallowed time, an ex-quisitely exhilarating season for us. Our young family was dedi-cated to the celebration in the fullest sense. We decked the halls with boughs of chains made from the faded green and red of school art paper. We decorated Yule logs for the neighbors, adding ribbons and cones, sparklers, and wee bags of colored flame powder. A note explained the tradition of the log. We put suet and cranberries out for the birds and covered every pane of glass with a scissor-snipped snowflake. We stuffed and sugared dates, frosted and sampled cookies, popped and "strangled" the corn, as the children always said. We tossed tinsel toward the tree, and it fell to earth on the carpet, the hassock, the candlesticks, the Jell-o (tinsel and Easter grass seem to find their way into everything). We sang the carols, every verse of every one. Our own nativity play was at once pitiful and charming. A birthday cake for Baby Jesus was solemnly candled and joyfully cut. And we capped off the celebration reading from Luke by the light of a gentle hearth fire.

Every Christmas it was the same wonderful sameness.

Yet every Christmas was different, too. It snowed or it didn't. The homemade clay pot cracked or it didn't. Someone had measles or miraculously all were well at once. The tree was pulled over by the newest toddler or it somehow survived. But it was Christmas, and we didn't let anything spoil the feel of it.

The Christmas of 1951 we did it all again. Finally, Santa had come in the still of the night, and in the chill of the dawn our own destroying angels—four in a row—had descended upon their gifts. It was an all-day exercise in the futility of organization. How do you organize who is going to want which toy when?

The house was a delightful disaster area.

And I was in labor!

Surely the baby wouldn't come this early and ruin our Christmas day, I protested with alarm. Surely not.

Just as surely as I turned over the thought, I learned the lesson that I was not in charge of such sacred happenings after all. For that Christmas season the days were accomplished that I should be delivered and bring forth our fifth-born child. The hospital staff had been reduced to holiday proportions, and someone accused us of not having planned very well.

Ah! I admitted that. But then, how could our planning match

the plans of God anyway? Why, with his timing I was turned into a Mary for a moment. For unto us a child was born. When I first looked at her, my joy was so great. No season before had matched this one. I cradled her close to my heart and wondered and wept that Mary could survive seeing her Christmas child crucified on a cross.

Christmas ruined? No, Christmas forever after blessed; for a baby born at this season is a glorious gift. We named ours Holly. Grandmother insisted we couldn't call a child a shrub. But we could and we did, tacking on Jennifer to pacify grandparents and add dignity for genealogical records. But Holly is what we called her, and the name fit. *Holly* means happiness, and that's what she has brought to us all these years.

You see, we have celebrated the Christmas season with greater reverence since Holly's birth. The crèche became important. Artwork of the Holy Family took precedence over meaningless decor. The children learned the difference between the Savior and Santa Claus. We had a Christmas baby of our own that grew and waxed strong in spirit, reminding us again each year of the real reason for celebration and of why we love Christmas so much.

Actually, though, the hospital is really no place to spend the winter holidays if you have a choice. Several times in my life I have had no choice. And every time it has been some kind of an adventure.

The first time, I was seventeen.

Carolers had long since sung and gone. Visitors had presented their poinsettias and returned to their own celebrations. The doctor pagings came over the speaker so softly now that only the night nurse could discern the details. The whole hospital was tuned way down in its customary nighttime pattern.

Only it wasn't a customary night. It was Christmas Eve, and I was trapped there after surgery in a world dedicated to the grim realities of living and dying.

I was too young to die.

But was it living to be so lonely? so homesick for one's own bed, family, and familiar festivities in this most beloved season?

It was not. Of that I was sure. It was agony, and the hurt in my heart at that moment surpassed any pain from my incision.

One is always the child at Christmas, but my current situation nurtured only immaturity. I wailed and wallowed in self-pity.

That didn't help.

I pretended I was home in bed and pressed my eyes tight against the distractions of flickering flashes from the emergency call-board out in the hall.

That didn't help either. An alive mind conjures up images more clear than eyes can see.

If only I could go to sleep. I squeezed my eyes harder.

Christmas Eve was always a sleepless night. There is much tossing and turning, restlessly rumpling the bedclothes and snuggling down again in a vain effort to bury the body in the comfort of quilts. Turning on the tummy to silence a pounding heart. Turning on the back to deliberately give way to wild speculations of Santa's plans. Then shifting to the side to calmly, quietly, concentrate on the faintest, far-away Christmas sound.

I couldn't even turn over now. But I could move my arms!

As quickly as the thought crossed my mind, action followed. I doubled my fist and pushed with all my might against the wall behind my head and sent my wheeled bed scooting out from the corner to a fine place right before the window.

What joy!

No Bethlehem looked more welcome to the Wise Men than Salt Lake City's mid-avenues looked to me that night.

Out there was Christmas.

This was an unfamiliar neighborhood, but the preparations were the same: Tree lights still on in many front rooms. A dim bulb marking Santa's workshop in an attic, a basement, or a storage porch. Dark stretches in between where little ones wrestled with temptation to peek at the proceedings, doing their own restless tossing and turning, their own kind of sweet suffering.

All those people beyond my world excitedly going through the rituals of Christmas just as we did it at our house. And all the bright dawnings that would follow!

I was amazed at the new, broader perspective.

I stared. I stretched my sore body for a better view. I heaped my heart into those houses with the lights still shining so far after midnight. I sighed a nice sigh. I didn't feel lonely anymore. There were people out there making Christmas happen.

Suddenly certain yearnings welled up within me. I had always been such a taker. I had been sleepless at Christmas, wondering what I would get. Tonight I had been sleepless because I felt left out. But out there others were sleepless with the preparation of giving.

When the night nurse came in on her routine rounds, she was irate because my bed was out of position.

"But it's Christmas out there," I feebly explained, as she pushed my bed back to the corner. "I need it to be Christmas in here."

Then I begged her to do me a favor in the silent of the night. I had a table-sized Christmas tree that friends had brought and decorated. It was my corner of Christmas and I loved it because it helped dispel my holiday gloom. But now I could use it well. Now I had something to give.

The night nurse smiled as she carried my little pine tree down the hall as a Christmas surprise to the child from out of town.

And I settled down at last for a long Christmas nap.

Sometimes at this season a person has to be well to survive the hospital. The staff is pared. People are anxious about their own celebrating. All kinds of things can happen.

One year I entered the hospital, a long week before Christmas, with a baby on the way (overdue at that), and something went mighty wrong.

It was 1947, and one hundred years had passed since the pioneers had crossed the Great Plains. As Salt Lakers, we were very involved in that centennial celebration for the community.

My husband and I and two children under three, with this current baby on the way, traced that pioneer trek from Nauvoo to Salt Lake. Only we did it by automobile and for the purpose of setting up the campsites and preparing the public for the commemorative trekkers who would follow. Those trekkers would be reenacting the first Mormon movement west, duplicating as much as possible the food, the clothing, and the life-styles of those hardy folks one hundred years before. Only they would do it by car, too, with covered wagon replicas mounted on top and on each side.

All the way across the plains, at the gravesites and historical markers and through the mountain passes, I thought of those pioneer women — my own ancestors — bearing their babies in wagon bottoms, at best. There was nothing to help ease the pain. There was little to comfort if trouble developed and nothing to do but bury the baby in the sagebrush and leave it behind on the trail if the infant didn't take hold.

And sometimes the mother was buried too.

Being with child myself, with toddlers alongside, I was empathetic in a way that Sunday School lessons had never helped me to be.

But now it was December, and I lay in the comfort of the hospital with a problem that couldn't have happened to those mothers of newborns back then.

They had brought me the wrong baby!

My husband had finished writing a book about the trek just in time to rush me to the hospital. I fell all the way down the steps in my rush to give him the word that it was time. The child was overdue, and the signals were critical. All of which hastened the arrival of ten-pound Christine. I had her *au naturel*, whether I liked it or not, and felt ashamed the whole time at my suffering, remembering those pioneer heroines.

When they brought me my baby for the first time, I smiled in grand pride the way mothers do. Such a wonder! Only a good-sized lump before, and seconds later a new being in the history of womankind. But as I snuggled her to me, a strange feeling came over me. This bundle wasn't mine.

I had scarcely seen her at the time of the birth, so I couldn't base the feeling on her appearance. Deep inside me a faint stirring began that there had been a mistake. I went back to the nursing, only to have the feeling well up within me again. This time I chalked it up to guilt — all those pioneer mothers who buried their babies in the cause of religious freedom for the gospel of Jesus Christ, and here I was in warmth, etc., etc., etc. I scolded myself.

But the feeling wouldn't be quelled.

This baby was not mine.

I checked the name tag against my own bracelet tag. They matched. I undressed the infant — a girl. Okay. Then I read the name taped on her back. *Cannon*. The name tallied. The room number was correct, too. Settle down, Elaine. What more do you want?

My own baby.

The more I tried putting it out of my mind, chalking my mood up to "plain fever" or Christmas hysteria or new-mother fatigue, the more sure I was that this child, though darling, belonged to somebody else.

And somebody else had mine.

So with my heart pounding by now and my ears buzzing with the throb, I rang for the nurse. I told her my problem. She went through the checking ritual of tags and tape as I had done already.

She explained that I was still groggy from anesthetic and would feel better at the next feeding. And that I should be thankful I had a baby at all. *She* didn't.

"But I'm not groggy. I didn't have anesthetic. She came much too fast," I said. "And I know she isn't mine," I added lamely.

The more she tried to silence me, to explain away my uneasiness, the harder my heart pounded, assuring me that I was right and she was wrong.

She lost her patience, her nurse's cool. There was nothing to do but what any red-blooded woman would do, pioneer or not, who responds to her spiritual promptings and is frustrated—I cried.

The nurse was greatly annoyed. Disgusted might be a better word. She swept up that baby out of my arms and that was the last I saw of any baby through the next two feeding periods.

Now, I love all babies, but if I had any choice in the matter I'd rather have my own. So I called my doctor. He was unavailable. I called my pediatrician. He had the day off. I called my husband, who couldn't be reached. Hours passed, a constant prayer in my mind and fear filling my heart. Finally, I called the hospital director at his home. Now, when you hit a man where he works, it hurts. A crying woman, insisting she has been given the wrong baby—and at Christmas—is trouble. And that director came at once, even if it was after hours.

Fortunately, at that time a baby's footprints were taken in that hospital while the infant was still connected to the mother. When the comparisons were made, it was proven that the baby I had been given wasn't mine. The *Cannon* tape had been inadvertently put on the wrong one of two babies born at the same time during that sacred season of celebration. Hours later, when at last I was given a baby to feed, a peace settled upon me. I cared not for tags and tapes. The Spirit assured me that she was mine. When I look at her now, a mother herself, with every physical trait that marks her as ours for sure, I smile to myself. Oh, she's proved me right, of course, as footprints did long ago. But faith and the Spirit and God's help with the unknown are part of the wonderful adventure of Christmas.

Strange Blame
on the Season

When Jesus was born, legend tells us, the sun danced in the sky. Leaves burst forth on bare trees, and fruit ripened out of season. Gnarled olive trees straightened, and voiceless birds sang. Such was the wonder of change at his coming.

Our own lives feel freshened and ripened as Christmas works its magic. Year after year we are willing partakers. We stand a little straighter ourselves before our ugly burdens. We sprout qualities we didn't know we had in dealing splendidly with our fellows.

While we learn and grow, though, we may stir up a trait or two in the name of Christmas kindness that can cast a strange blame on the season.

I first became aware of this one wintry day as I sat by the little arched fireplace in our living room watching the huge lump of coal glow into embers. I was young and I had been reading a new book I'd received for Christmas — Dale Carnegie's *How to Win Friends and Influence People*. Santa was always trying to help me. But it worked. I got a new insight into giving.

Carnegie gave advice about being a people pleaser. It was a new dimension on the old Golden Rule principle of treating others as you'd like to be treated that interested me. Carnegie said that if you are going fishing and you want to catch fish, you don't take your own favorite food for bait — say, strawberries and cream. You take worms, the favorite food of fish.

So if you want to win friends, I interpreted, you don't feed people your favorite things, you feed them theirs. Great! That goes for music, books, compliments, conversations, and love. You don't just treat others as you yourself like to be treated, you treat them as *they* like to be treated.

I was about twelve then, and a true believer. I determined then and there to quit giving my brother *Bomba, the Jungle Boy* books just so I could read them. He was long past the age for them, and giving them to him because I wished someone would give them to me didn't make *his* Christmas happy.

A more dramatic witness of this principle came to me much later in life when we were young marrieds, surrounded by echoes of ourselves in a suburban subdivision.

With the remarkable inefficiency of some young marrieds, Esther had borne a houseful of babies in quick succession. It wasn't what she had had in mind when she and Rudy fell in love, but it is what happened to them anyway. They had met and married, later moving from an obscure farm town at the edge of nowhere to our neighborhood. Esther was musically gifted. Rudy was too fragile for the farm. Moving to the city seemed the answer. He could go to school. She could teach piano. Esther had it all planned.

But she was always pregnant, always diapering, always playing for somebody's funeral. Rudy was always at school, always studying, always doing odd jobs.

One winter it all caught up with them.

The household was in chaos. Esther was so ill she couldn't teach or play or get with child. Something was terribly wrong.

The children had always struggled pretty much after themselves, so that didn't change; but now, without Esther's teaching, there would be no money for anything. Rudy finally quit school to take another job, and Esther went into surgery two days before Christmas.

Then a startling thing happened. Word was passed of Esther's problem. We neighbors stepped in to help — with our can of worms.

A home without a parent is vulnerable. This one, too, was now open for inspection — up for critical grabs. Its evidence lay bare for every woman on the block who came forth to "help."

"Hey!" called one, "take a look at this fridge. You'd have to keep a mouse on leash to find the cheese!"

"Can you believe this bathroom? It ought to be declared a disaster area."

"Poor thing."

"A pitiful situation."

"How can people live this way?"

"Cluck, cluck. Tsk, tsk."

Gossip and judgment are unkind companions.

Someone decided a massive clean-up, fix-up, paint-up was just what Esther's place needed. With Christmas shining in our hearts, we pitched in to prepare a surprise. The children were sworn to secrecy, husbands hauled in to help, and the family Christmas was dismantled at once.

Rudy kept on working his sixteen-hour day.

Each room was a different color, so each room now was attacked with well-meaning vengeance. Each room was now scoured and scrubbed and painted clean white. And talked about all over town.

Pictures were rehung the way the do-gooders saw fit. Cupboards were rearranged for a stranger's kitchen habits. The children's treasures were boxed and shifted to the basement. The schedules on the bulletin board were scrapped in the interest of aesthetics. Books were reshelved in alphabetical order, and the children's growth progress marks in the hall were painted forever away.

Then Esther came back, and the neighbors, blessedly, went away.

A few weeks later the family moved, taking us all quite by surprise. They moved on the day of the heaviest storm of that year. The snow was so thick it whitened everything—reminiscent of those rooms that had been changed from the colors the family loved to the white someone thought looked so clean. Esther loved color, and she reminded us of that on moving day by flying bright-colored streamers of crepe paper from the car's door handles, hood decor, radio antenna, and fenders. They drove back of the moving van in a flurry of color and crepe paper down the street and out of our lives. And they honked all the way.

They moved because the house wasn't home anymore. Like deciduous trees bared of their leaves, like Christ on the cross, their family home had been laid naked before their neighbors and found wanting. Oh, they had been "done unto," but not after the manner of Christ or Carnegie.

With infinite kindness coupled with caring, may we do our good deeds so that we create a Christmas of joy rather than placing a strange blame upon the season.

Caught in the spell of good will toward men, I learned to lie at Christmas. I was very young when I realized "honesty is the best policy." Principle had to be set aside on occasion. I just couldn't bear to see anyone disenchanted. I didn't dare admit disappointment before my parents when Santa's surprises were surveyed. I believed in the system. Even at its worst, Christmas was better than any other day of the year. Still, it could be made better if people would only try a little harder or learn a little more.

The parade up and down the blocks to see what was beneath each tree was an annual Christmas morning tradition for the children in our neighborhood. How parents permitted such an abomination of the day, such a trial-by-comparison trauma, I can't understand. But year after year the parade persisted.

The gifts beneath the trees in the homes of my friends were as different as the income and situation, as the taste and concern for the celebration, would allow. And in the difference there was always pain for somebody.

That's how I learned to lie, and that's a strange blame to place on the season.

What people received for Christmas didn't declare their happiness nor determine their popularity (a term we used a lot then and which in our circle was practically synonomous with happiness). You see, the girl whose family was hardest hit in the depression got the least for Christmas. But she was the best loved. And the girl who got too much suffered one more rejection.

One Christmas we traipsed into the home of the girl who always got too much. We entered, surveyed, and gasped. Gift after gift was shown to us. When she finally displayed the little pearl ring in a velvet box, we all just looked away. You can't eat pearls and they won't keep you warm, and that was what gift-giving was all about in those times. But this girl felt our rejection, and the Christmas light went out in her eyes. My child's heart tightened with the snap of the lid of the velvet ring box. "It's beautiful," I said. That was no lie. But then I continued, "I wish I had one, too." That was the lie. I said it not out of greed but out of goodwill. I hoped it would give her a friend. But the ring was the final blow that set her apart from the others. It was too much, much too marvelous, and it made her someone they couldn't quite be.

Maybe it wasn't the ring that brought the rejection, maybe it was the flaunting of all the fringe benefits of having a father who had a job, but she changed after that. I never saw her wear that ring — even to Sunday School — after that.

There was a friend in that pitiful parade whose father gave her a pair of shoes every year. Period. Shoes. Every year he would choose them himself without her counsel, and every year they'd be sturdy enough to last forever, ugly enough to ruin a girl's chances at life. She hated them, of course, and we hated him for what it did to her. Christmas after Christmas. That's how I learned to lie, too, by telling her they were okay, cute, neat, or great (in whatever the vernacular of the year), hoping against hope it would help.

Then there was the girl who didn't even get a gift as grand as shoes. Except maybe an apron her aunt had made, she seldom received anything at all. As we neared her house she'd begin talking grandly about how she had all her gifts put away already. There was no point in even going to her house, she'd insist. But everybody else persisted just the same.

"Let's go to your house last," I'd suggest, hoping we'd all have to go home by then. And sometimes it worked.

I loved this friend with a protective passion and gave her the best gift on my list. For we *had* to exchange gifts. That's what friends at Christmas were for. And I lied to her each time by telling her all I wanted was a bottle of her Mom's applesauce. And that's what she gave me, ribbon-tied.

I think of that each canning season now, wondering why my own applesauce never tastes like the memory.

One Christmas I was sick and suffering puppy love pangs, all at once. I couldn't "parade," and my self-pity was disgusting. But late in the day my boyfriend showed up by my bed with a little spaniel puppy his mother had made from white yarn. It was softly stuffed, button-eyed—a treasure forever. "It's funny!" I lied, and struggled to laugh before I cried. For that toy from that boy was the most beautiful gift I'd ever had.

And he lied back, "Oh, it's nothing. It's dumb!" But that didn't shadow the pride in his eyes.

For he'd given to please, and I'd received it in the same spirit. And that's the wonder of Christmas.

"To Every Thing
a Season"

The winter Stanley killed himself was the first time personal death seemed a real possibility to me. He was just our age and had hanged himself from the hot water pipe crossing the ceiling of their basement apartment. If it could happen to Stanley . . .

Everyone who had ignored him in life was curiously interested in him at death. People crowded the funeral, but the few berried boughs plus the funeral wreath from the bishop did little to dispel the gloom.

No one knew where Stanley's father was. Mother said maybe that was one reason his Mom carried on so. Daddy said she didn't know any better, since they never came to church. Anyway, her sobs and wails railed against my ear and assaulted my heart. She hung over his coffin, clinging to his poor stiff body, flattening the paper lilies as she struggled to hold him to her. She kept calling him "My baby," and the bishop kept tugging at her shoulders, mumbling, "Come, sister."

I lingered, frankly staring. I wondered how I could help. For I yearned to help, to heal her, to remind her that her son would be just fine with Heavenly Father. She was much older than I, but it seemed she hadn't learned that yet. Besides, I couldn't figure out why she fought so frantically for a boy who had chosen to leave her. All the sobs in the kingdom wouldn't open his eyes or bring her another chance to rectify her neglect of him. Anyway, if he weren't already dead, he'd have suffocated under her heavy black veils drowned in Evening in Paris. She was the first woman I'd ever seen up close who wore rouge like that.

"To every thing there is a season," the bishop said at last, "a time to get and a time to lose." That mother's moans punctuating Ecclesiastes wounded me—not because she had lost Stanley, but because Stanley had been driven to death. It was all wrong. Life was to be lived with whatever options. Grieving at the grave was ill-timed. I believe it was then that I experienced deep inside me my first sweet response to blessing counting.

Brother Richmond taught a lesson on the Resurrection the next Sunday, and while he never had more rapt attention, it wasn't until Betty's sister LaPreal died of sleeping sickness a couple of years later that we learned of dignity in death. The peace of that service was its own defense for good living.

One winter the man across the street brought home a new mother for his children. She had never been married before, and we wondered at her stenographer's clothes and her sleek Carole Lombard hairdo. She didn't seem up to the brood of boys who ran around half-dressed and barefoot on rainy days and sultry spells alike. Mother often commented that in spite of their casual ways those children didn't have the sickness we did.

We could see their property from our sun porch, as we called it, and we'd press our noses against the glass to watch their adventures in a tree house with its own rope swing and a dugout in the field for potato bakes. The father seemed to be gone a lot after the first while. How she managed inside we could only imagine, but outside the boys paid no heed to her gentle pleas.

In time she changed—hair, figure, clothes, demeanor. Some toddlers of her own swelled the ranks of the family and the size of her hips. Then one day she died. It was interesting to watch the way those boys shaped up in such a hurry. They carried her coffin, ordered flowers to be sent, and took the younger children in hand. What it amounted to was that she was missed. By the time the McMasters had finished singing "In the Garden" at the funeral, those boys were all bawling.

Some people dismissed her death as a blessing and a deserved rest, but the family found that they had lost their best friend. What they hadn't done for her in life they hustled to do for her in death. Their place took on a shine at last, but it seemed to me it was too little too late, and so for nearly a week I helped Mother with the dishes without being told.

Ready for Winter

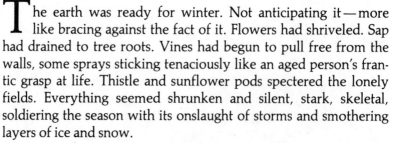

The earth was ready for winter. Not anticipating it—more like bracing against the fact of it. Flowers had shriveled. Sap had drained to tree roots. Vines had begun to pull free from the walls, some sprays sticking tenaciously like an aged person's frantic grasp at life. Thistle and sunflower pods spectered the lonely fields. Everything seemed shrunken and silent, stark, skeletal, soldiering the season with its onslaught of storms and smothering layers of ice and snow.

It was after autumn's colorful exit, after the teasing frost of early November nights and before nature was used to its own demise. Everything, even the evergreens, was closed up, pinched, packed, laced, locked, and ready for winter.

But sometimes the waiting went on. Sometimes the season never came to its full, like a single person never mellowed by marriage.

Like Allie.

Allie was a hopelessly crippled arthritic who seemed forever destined to be alone, cushioned in her big chair, pounding walnuts open with a rock on a breadboard. She couldn't grip another kind of tool, so she hammered and pried her days away, awkwardly flicking the nut meat free with a fat-handled ice pick.

And that was Allie's life — winter-wracked.

Until we moved in next door.

Allie lived with her sister in a bungalow surrounded by hundreds of tulips that had been left in the ground so long they had reverted to basic yellow. The quiet the sisters had known before we became neighbors disappeared when six children and a dog promptly made a path through the tulips, the hyacinths, the phlox, and the petunias in turn of bloom. And that first year, waiting for winter, we trampled the stems and stubble as well going to their door. Next spring there would be a proper path built, but meanwhile, no complaints, just a warm welcome.

We all loved visiting them, but it was Tony who really eased Allie's pitiful brace against winter. And Allie accomplished the miracle of proving how early a child can learn all manner of marvelous things if he is taught from the beginning in patience and love.

It all began the day the heavens finally released their load upon the waiting world. Snow, the great common denominator, equalized everything white. When the storm stopped and there were no more snowflakes to watch out of the window, the children made frantic preparations to get outside. The bundling began. Leggings. Mittens. Mufflers. Caps. Sweaters under coats. Dad's old socks over shoes and under galoshes. One slips a child into a waterproof zip suit these days, but then it was a long process to find winter swaddlings for six.

Meanwhile, Tony, our toddler, well under two, couldn't wait for his turn at the dressing. I felt a cold draft from the open door before I missed him. His tiny footprints in the snow with a stumble or two clearly visible marched right to Allie. I followed the trail and the scramble marks up the steps to the door. There through the front window I could see them already at play. Her head bent to meet his as she pointed out letters, taught him simple songs, explained life.

I was grateful to find him bundled against the wet and cold, but we had to agree upon some ground rules.

No one must be imposed upon. Allie's strength must be preserved. Tony's mother must know of his whereabouts. His schedule had to be protected. But even these faltered finally in the face of Allie's need and Tony's hunger to learn.

Some said, "Don't you care that he wants to be there with her so much?" (Rather than with you, they implied.)

Care? I wondered at the question. How can we be so blessed? was a more accurate reading of my feelings. There was no way I could have given him that kind of attention just them. My life was so pressured and energy so spent. Five children in a row had come along almost as fast as they could. Then finally, some time later, Tony came, the second son we had been promised. This child was special because of circumstances too sacred to relate here, and I did not want the ordinary demands of motherhood to deprive him of the personal attention he ought to have.

Allie was an answer to my prayers.

What her body lacked in mobility, her mind made up for in creativity. Little "people" were torn from bits of paper. Moistened with a finger on the tongue, they came alive to ride a pipe cleaner horse, perform on a box stage, sail in a walnut shell, star in a game of letters. All the while, principles were being taught about goodness and greatness, giving but sharing, too.

Allie was a bountiful benefit to Tony. In time she bloomed like the apple trees in our orchard, signaling that winter was finally done with.

As he grew he brought her things from his world outside — a spider in a glass jar captured at fall's edge; snowflakes on a pie tin hurried inside before they could melt; a bird's egg fallen from the horse chestnut tree; rocks, scrubbed and ready for her to choose a favorite from; and endless "writings" he had scribbled at home.

One day Allie made a grammatical error which Tony corrected in a comfortable way each had become used to.

"That bird's egg looks lovely speckled like that, don't it?"

"Donuts are what you eat," was his reply. Then he picked up the egg to check the speckles while she smiled.

The heart knows no barriers, suffers no generation gap. So they grew together these two, through the winters when a child was bored at home and Allie was trapped in her cushions. He awaited the storms and the times inside with Allie. And when spring came he would often sit with her on the porch in the evening while the stars were counted and the moths were explained and his wonder in the world increased.

Then early one spring, quite suddenly, while Tony was still young, Allie died in her sleep. Her winter was over. We wept with the rain that this precious chapter was finished. Weeping endures only for the night, and joy does come in the morning, for Tony's life had been influenced and Allie's heart had known love.

She spoke softly. He is a man now, but so does he.

She moved gently. Tony does, too.

Sometimes when the snowstorm is heavy with soft flakes that cover the ground quickly, I think of Allie all those long years ago and the mothering she and I shared.

And I thank God for her.

It is easy to thank God for this friend and for other friends, for adventures, awakenings, miracles.

I know God and love him because of my father. He had great faith. He also was fine looking, fine behaving, athletic, and appealing. He was a tender and loving human being. God was male. Therefore he must be fine looking, fine behaving, tender, loving, and lovable. So I loved him after that simple reasoning of childhood.

And it has worked for me ever since.

It worked for me even when my father finally lay dying. It was one of those teasing November days when we wait for earth's demise, and we waited, too, now for Daddy to cross over the line into the land of light.

It was my turn to keep vigil his last day. He wafted in and out of reality early in the morning. Then later he became very still for a long time. I wiped blood from his lips and poured love back into his spirit. Then suddenly he awakened singing a little song Mother had written to him just before they were married. That voice so dear—model for my early ventures into harmony—sang while the tears spilled from his eyes. I watched in silence, in wonder, in love for him such as I had never known before, my heart pounding and swelling and filling my whole being. And I felt love come back. With Dad, love was always an exchange.

He alternated between stillness and struggling. Did he know who was beside him? He didn't respond now to my voice. But he reached . . .

Reaching for my hand, are you, Dad? How shyly you reach, tentatively. Is this what those fluttering lids are saying . . . embarrassed a little to admit that you have such a mighty need, like a child might have? Reach, Dad. Dying isn't easy. What's wrong with a need to hold on? A need for reassurance that you aren't all alone. It's a privilege, Dad, to hold your hand in your last days like you did mine in my first. "Except we become as little children we can in no wise enter the kingdom of heaven." Christ told us that. You know. You were first to tell me. And how many times you've said something like that in recent years! So reach, childlike and needful. You're nearing those gates. But remember, though I am holding your hand, you still are doing the leading. I'll gladly give you my hand and once more, one more time, you can lead me ever closer to the presence of God.

I left the hospital then, with Dad in the care of his loving son.

My heart was heavy awaiting this winter in our lives, yet I marveled at the sweet feeling that angels were hovering near in that room and at the wonder of hearing him speak happily to his sisters long gone but so dearly cherished. It was like sun on the snowbanks, this mixed blessing of death for a loved one who was suffering.

In this tender mood I approached my home only to be greeted by a distraught woman awaiting my return. She had come unannounced for help and was completely insensitive to my mood, suddenly spilling forth a tirade of troubles.

I sublimated my own needs and listened to her intently, even prayerfully. Though her problem was real, its solution seemed so clear.

When she stopped to sip the warm broth I'd placed beside her, my faith surfaced.

I spoke with fervor born out of my experience, "Oh, my dear, don't you know that God lives?"

"Of course I know God lives!" She hurled the words at me. "He just doesn't know that *I* live."

So we talked about this while the wind whistled its power and the trees simply bent slightly to weather the storm.

Her prayers hadn't been answered just as she thought they should have. Therefore, God wasn't aware of her and her needs, she reasoned. I told her about my father who lay dying at that moment with the Spirit encircling him in a sacred peace. As at birth, I described. There is a spirit pervading the whole process of birth and of death, if we'll tune ourselves to it. It is peaceful, holy, and puts a burning in the bosom.

"And there ought to be a spirit pervading our living," I added thoughtfully. "Oh, God lives. And he knows we live, too. He knows when our hearts are breaking and our defenses are down. But he waits to be gracious before warming our wintry days. We aren't likely to find him rudely barging in on our free agency when our backs are turned to him."

I remembered now and told her how the Capitol gardener of my youth had shown me a flower and told me to hold it just so and the leaves would turn to the light, and that if I did that with my life I would see a miracle. I suggested she try that herself.

So she went away mellowed and thoughtful, her hard heart melted like post-seasonal snows when the sun comes out full light.

Living is sometimes harder than dying, but it wasn't that way with my friend Marie. She lived with deep joy in her husband and seven children, in her mountain home and city place, with a host of friends who basked in her serenity. She was peace personified, and she nurtured her relationships like the herbs and flowers in her gardens — a little tender feeling here, a little cutting off there. In other words, she was in control of things and made her choices with the confidence of one who knows which is the best road for her to travel. Like the fact that she almost always wore a handsome white tailored shirt and an appropriate skirt for any and all occasions. A closet full of clothing was a useless extravagance. Her favorite shopping was done in the toy shops of the exotic places they traveled to so frequently, while friends would haunt dress shops and gift boutiques.

When the last child was still an infant, Marie waited for her winter to pass. She had cancer and had struggled through the agonies of treatment and prolonged hospitalization. We had had a pleasant visit with her that last day. She spoke casually of funerals and children and God's way of making us learn. She talked of "Equanimity" and "God's hidden blessings." On the wall of her private room we had flashed slides of our trips together — a rerun of life, you might say. Marie made it so easy for us in our awkward efforts at compassion. We came to help but she was the lifter, the comforter, the patient and peaceful one.

In her typical way Marie had become interested in a good woman who scrubbed and cleaned unusually well around her room. The visits were so rewarding there. She was cleaning to earn extra money to buy her missionary son another suit.

Marie's husband provided well for her. She could have reached into her bedside table for a checkbook and written an amount to help the housekeeper with her project. But, instead, when the woman had left, Marie picked up the phone to call her husband and tell him the story. "I thought you would like to know about this," she explained, "in case there is something you want to do about it."

Those were about the last words he heard her say, for she

suffered a heart attack right after. When he asked me to speak at her funeral, he told me to tell about the woman in need and Marie's final call to him.

"It about sums up our life together," the heartbroken man explained. "She was my eyes, my ears, my heart, and she let me do the doing. It was her wonderful way of being womanly that I'll miss."

Being womanly is not reserved for young wives only, just as winter in a life is no respecter of persons. I have a friend who is past ninety who is truly womanly and, old as she is, she refuses to complain about the seasons. She has known a lot of winters, and the springs in her life surely are limited, but her way of getting ready for what comes next is to go on doing something useful with the time she has. One day I drove down the hill by our home in a terrible knee-deep snowstorm. There was Leah standing at the bus stop, bundled against the cold. I stopped my car and asked her to get in and let me drive her to where she was going. She refused. I explained that my car had snow tires and I had experience in driving through storms. That didn't seem to convince her to get in either. Finally, I got out of my car and went over to help her, "Come on, Leah. Where are you going? Please, let me take you there." At last she admitted that she was on her way to do volunteer duty at the new baby ward of the hospital several miles away. "I'll take you there. My car will make it easily," I urged her. I hooked my arm through hers to guide her toward my car, but she shook it free and smiled sadly, "Elaine, it is so important that those precious new babies get rocked. They don't cry so much and they get good loving when I hold them. If I let you take me to the hospital by car today, I am so old that tomorrow I will forget how to get there on the bus. I had better just stand here and wait till the bus comes."

And some of us just stand and wait our lives away or brace ourselves against hard times. Others, I've learned, take hold of their lives, work with their happenings. And, ready for winter or not, they'll do something wonderful with the time they have on earth.

Summer

For, lo, the winter is past, the rain is over and gone; the flowers appear on the earth; the time of the singing of birds is come.

(Song of Solomon 2:11, 12.)

Summer on
the Hill

There is in summer a continuum imperceptibly marking the shift from year to year, age to age, wisdom to wisdom. Summer is the only time which is enough to learn all the things that can't be taught in the classroom.

When I was an infant we moved to 391 Wall Street on Capitol Hill. The Hill was set apart by the natural boundaries of Ensign Peak, City Creek Canyon, and Main Street sloping into town. Our houses clustered about the massive Utah State Capitol, making our neighborhood unique, tight-knit, and highly motivating.

It was before land developers, so the houses on the Hill were individual—like the people inside. The split shake shingle with its brooding overhangs and the simple facsimile of a French chateau mingled comfortably with the red brick bungalow, the Christmas-card cottage, and the pioneer cabin remodeled for another generation's needs. The only apartment was a haphazard affair constructed before the advent of building restrictions, but it broadened our experience with a transient element that some grownups resisted.

The people on the Hill were largely Mormon. Some conformed to strict standards. Some did not. But they all showed up for every groundbreaking, funeral, three-act play, and missionary farewell on the schedule at the meetinghouse.

Living on the Hill was a child's paradise where summer was a rare blend of the mysteries of the wilderness and sophistications of a capital city. We scaled peaks and the rickety ladder to the Capitol dome in equal excitement. We became conscious of flag ceremonies and the poignancy of "Taps" at sunset long before we could tie our own sneakers. We explored caves one day and the silent chambers of the Senate the next. We became friends with the Governor and the gardener alike. We hounded the state chemist, keeper of countless glass tubes, but we learned more about sanitation by studiously avoiding wading in City Creek. Signs posted everywhere along its winding route reminded that this was the water we drank and nobody's feet were declared clean enough!

We were taught early that for us meadowlarks warbled, "Salt Lake City is a pretty little place," and that if worse came to worst, we, like the pioneers who settled this valley, could exist on the roots of the sego lilies dotting the brown slopes behind the Capitol.

Summers on Capitol Hill held special compensation for a city child. Though we didn't have the company of cows, horses, and roosters to crow in the dawn, we did have the Capitol lions. These great creatures that guarded the east and west entrances to the edifice were frankly considered our private property.

How we would clamber over those lions, stretching ourselves cool over the bony backs. We'd examine the haunches, the tails, the claws. We'd finger the eyes and rule the world from our perch behind the great mane. Though they were just cast cement, it was only on our truly brave days that we dared edge our way up front to scrunch under the jaws and sit in the circle of the forelegs. Sometimes we'd feast on our supply of stale Easter eggs kept hidden in a secret place for emergencies.

When we wearied of lions, we'd descend upon the confines of the Capitol itself. First we'd prowl the dark ground-level with its case after case of stuffed buffalo and coyotes, of prize-winning Utah grains, and produce displayed in enormous fancy glass jars that enhanced the appearance of the product considerably but never made us hungry.

Or we'd do a few somersaults on the brass railings guarding the giant black block of Utah bituminous coal, before brushing past the politicians to the sacred floors above. Visitors were awe-struck at the beauty of this building built in the days of early western settlements. We'd sit for hours studying the enormous murals at each end, depicting such heritage as was ours. The vast dome itself, painted with fleecy clouds, rivaled the sky for inspiration. The halls, the balconies, the balustrades with their cold iron eagles offered endless settings for fantasies that filled our young souls between Memorial and Labor days. Endless settings, inside and outside, all summer long. We knew it all so well!

We followed the guided tours so many times we could give the lectures ourselves by the time we turned ten. We knew how much gold leaf bathed the ornate walls of the formal reception room, and we were hard pressed sometimes to not jump the gun on the tour guide. And if he forgot, we were quick to point out the butterfly formed by the veining in one of the giant marble columns. Oh, those columns! They were so huge we could hug only half, and a child was well hidden at game.

Before heading for home, we would beg cigar boxes from the newsstand and make doll beds to drag around behind us on a long string. The stand man, in his funny red fez, would patiently poke a hole in the end of the box with his ice pick and supply us with great lengths of string. Once home, I had to either cover any trace of tobacco language on the box with magazine pictures or doilies or abandon the homemade doll bed, because Mother was adamant about our avoiding the very appearance of evil.

Sometimes in summer my family would picnic under the catalpa trees shading the Capitol's western slopes. We'd look out over the old section of Salt Lake City with its quaint-gabled, adobe brick houses and the beloved black Tabernacle, fat and squat like a potato bug, commanding its own place in the shadow of the pristine spires of the Holy House of the Lord (as we then called the temple on Temple Square). We took turns pointing out the kinds of trees and spelling the names and chorusing together at last that the first trees were carried across the plains to green-up the Salt Desert land our city had sprung from. Cottonwoods for shade, poplars to break the wind, mountain elm because they grew so fast.

Mother would tell us stories about her pioneer heritage so we would know we had "roots," until Daddy, bereft of ancestors who had crossed the plains, brought us back to reality with ambitious plans for the Capitol Hill Improvement League, he being its founder and president.

"Capitol Hill Improvement League," I invariably murmured to myself. How could this area be *improved*? Why, the Capitol, the grounds, the secret places and public face of it all proved our purposeful playground summer after summer. The hills and houses surrounding us were the kingdom of our delight and the seat of our best learnings. The people loved life and worked hard. Like Whitman's child that went forth, these things and these places and the people who happened there in that time—these became part of me in the stretching cycles of summer.

In the Season Thereof

The summer we painted the oleander was the beginning of a lifelong attitude about appropriateness. One doesn't gild the lily. One doesn't tamper with natural beauty.

An oleander in Utah was something of a novelty in those days. Ours was the family treasure. Daddy had invested something of himself in that plant. Some years before, he had packed it in soggy cotton and brought it on the long trip from California to his mother in Salt Lake City. When Grandmother died, it was ours and was the more valuable because it had been hers. It was nurtured, protected. Each winter, ceremoniously, it was swathed in burlap and hauled into the garage. Each time we climbed into the Studebaker it was at the command, "Don't crush the oleander." Each summer it was brought forth to be hosed down, pot-painted, and put in place by the porch. Then at last profuse blooms rewarded everyone.

On this particular day I was suffering — at age three — the tortures of rejection. There was some painting going on at our house and I had been programmed out. When the supplies were left unguarded, I sought to beautify the oleander. What sport!

What a sense of power I felt in changing the look of that shrub with each flamboyant slap of the brush until the shrieks of my parents awakened me to my mischief. It was not beautiful at all. It was ruined, its pitiful petals sticking together in extravagant blueness.

"One cannot improve on God," Daddy declared emphatically, shaking me soundly.

The oleander died, of course, but Daddy's counsel lives in me yet. A chair can be repainted to cover past damage, but a living, growing thing can be spoiled forever through witless tampering. And that goes for people as well as plants.

It was Daddy who would take my hand each spring and say, "Come along. It's time to see if there is a violet brave enough to weather the storms. Should we go see if summer is coming after all?" Then we'd gently brush aside sodden, left-over leaves in a sunny corner and always there would be a violet. Daddy was a wonder to me. He knew just when to look.

Of course, I grew up loving earth's green things, and in the season thereof they were plentiful and varied to us on the Hill because of the Capitol's spectacular offerings.

The formal gardens south of the Capitol fascinated me. There were trimmed hedges that spelled "Utah" and exotic blooms the home gardener could never afford. The gentle slopes so perfect for sleigh riding, Easter egg rolls, or somersaults in season were lined with cherry trees imported from distant Japan. All these were cared for by a gifted man who suffered from arthritis. We used to watch him wince when he stooped to cup new pansy plants into damp earth beds. He hobbled home from work past our house late each day, each step a new agony. No one questioned why he didn't change jobs. He was lucky to have one. But we were careful not to trample his gardens in thoughtless summer games.

One day I sat guarding our lemonade stand while Marilyn went for more ice chips. The street car would be along soon, and we almost always got some customers at this stop if there were ice chips in clean tin cups for the drink. I passed the time watching the gardener. He looked so hot, even from where I sat, and he moved like he hurt more than usual. Oh, I felt so sorry for him! Then I had a great idea. I'd treat him to some of our lemonade — free. It wasn't very cold but it was wet, and he'd know somebody cared about him. For safekeeping, I pocketed the pennies we'd taken in and stored in Mother's celluloid hair receiver. Then I crossed the street with the cup of lemonade.

"Well, thank you," he said, sipping it carefully. "You've added just enough sugar."

Some people downed their drinks in one gulp, so of course they couldn't tell if our mix was good or not. The gardener tasted it. He knew. Just as he knew which plants had the softest leaves and that my eyes were brown and not blue. He finished drinking and said that, since I had done him such a kind favor, he was going to do one for me — he was going to show me a kind of miracle. We walked over to the colorful bed of coleus plants, all dark red and green trimmed and velvety. He troweled one up and put it into my hands after interlocking my fingers so the soil wouldn't spill off the roots. I was to pot it, water it just so, and place it in a sunny window where I could watch "the miracle."

He took one ruffled leaf gently and, lifting it with his knobby fingers, said, "The coleus plant will lean to light. Turn your plant every two or three days and the leaves will turn right around again and lean to the light. Try it, Elaine. You'll see the miracle. And maybe it's something you'd like to do with your life."

No wonder we held him and his handiwork in a kind of reverence.

Heaven's Reach

The summer of sacrifice was the year everyone helped build the new stone chapel with contributions of labor or hard cash.

We had been meeting in the converted carriage house behind the McCune mansion, and the groundbreaking for our building was a celebration. So was the day the trucks dumped their loads of fieldstone on the site. We children had helped pay for those stones (bricks were too costly) by saving pennies in peanut butter jars, peddling needles and shoe laces door to door, or selling lemonade at the streetcar stops with the proceeds going for the cause. Edgar worked up a deal with the publishers of *Liberty* magazine and sold subscriptions. Mother was so impressed with his enterprising spirit that she signed up for two years. The sacrifice part came when someone suggested that instead of going downtown to the Saturday movie matinee, the children were to contribute their show money for stones.

Naturally, we were very interested in this project and hung

around the church lot across from the Capitol the better part of one summer.

The old stonemason had set up shop on the grounds and, being "hired" help from off the Hill, he was a unique being. He wore clothes that matched his scarred, stained hands which reflected years at his trade. He only shaved for Sunday. In utter fascination we watched the daily growth darken on his jawline and under his sharp nose. He didn't pay much attention to us children, but his young apprentice counted anything that breathed as his personal audience. The stonemason's hands were swift and sure, and it seemed he seldom rested from his labors. The apprentice, on the other hand, did a lot of leaning. Oh, he'd mix a little mortar or wheel a barrow full of stones to the workbench now and then, but mostly he just leaned, posturing and turning his bare, bronze body this way and that in the sun before our dazzled eyes.

The stonemason seldom spoke. The brash young apprentice knew all the filthy words to say and said them. Frequently. One day he was being especially coarse when the old man "finally got his dander up," as Mother would say when her temper flared. He raised his voice and announced solemnly: "No point in teaching these kids the ugly things when there are so many pretty things to talk about." And with a whap of his tool, the stonemason split a dull gray stone into colorful, shimmering halves ready to be mortared into walls. There was a sermon in those stones.

For me, from that day forward, the Capitol Hill Ward rose as a monument to the fact that you can't tell the inside of a thing by its covering—even with people.

This can be true of books too, I discovered in later years. Some of the fanciest bindings housed only trash. Some of the scroungiest-looking books spilled forth rare beauty, inspiration, and challenge.

For instance, one day in my early teens a boy slipped me a coverless collection of English verse with pages torn, worn, and soiled, but it changed my life. This passage was marked: "Ah, but a man's reach should exceed his grasp, or what's a heaven for?"

So wrote Browning decades before I read it fresh that day and took it personally, appropriate to my season of self-discovery, of hopeful idealism and firming philosophy. And I might never have reached if I'd been stopped by the cover.

That is another blessed blessing of summer — time enough to read and to know what you've read. I'd pick a few Italian plums from our tree and rub off the powdery white until the dark skins glistened red-purple. Then I'd retreat to the Capitol slope and read in the cool of sprinkler spray splashing off tree trunks, soon oblivious to the ka-chugging sound the rain-bird made.

In my summers I had romped through the Mark Tidd books and the Anne of Green Gables series, and had plowed through a Tarzan book or two just to please my brother. I had discovered the Lloyd C. Douglas books and dreamed of my own magnificent obsession. And I had fallen down Alice's rabbit hole and climbed Heidi's Alpine height seven or eight times by the summer I learned of Heaven's Reach and of the truth, one more time, about covers.

Worn leather volumes containing Shakespeare, Wordsworth, Longfellow, and Chaucer were passed into my hands by this boy who understood the grasp-and-reach theory. The public library provided me with ugly, stiff, practical new bindings of Dickens and Robert Louis Stevenson and Emerson's essay "Friendship" with the library number perforated across random pages. Then came the sharing of a simple maroon book called *Larry*, after the remarkable young man whose letters and journal entries and notes to Girl, his girl, were collected therein. We read that, and when he died in the end, almost before he had really lived, we wept.

I loved all these books unabashedly.

This boy and I couldn't understand everything we read, but it was so exhilarating trying to understand that it was like coming in with the tide. Stretching our minds in the reading and then struggling to say it back in our own words to each other kept our relationship going one swift summer and was the basis for a lifelong friendship.

48

We'd read and we'd walk and we'd sit on the curb and we'd talk. The reading, the matching of the masters against our Master, was sacred and stimulating business and fuel for the fires of friendship.

And I went through all that soul-soaring, and nobody in my family noticed what had happened to me. I was different inside but they went on treating me in the same old way around the house, just as my familiar drab "cover" dictated.

It was frustrating to me, and I tried to tell Mother about it one night. We sat on the porch in the dark, conscious of the cool cement beneath us. Somewhere "Harbor Lights" was being played. Somewhere a baby cried, and the Barton boy disturbed the night peace practicing his trumpet. Mother was so quiet when I stopped talking that I thought she didn't understand.

Then she said, "Well, I've always heard that the face you have when you are forty is exactly what you deserve. A person's cover comes quietly, Elaine, matching character only at the end, I believe. That's why it can be so cruel to judge others when you only see the outside of them."

Mother understood and I'm beginning to.

Minutiae

Summers I spent a lot of time sitting on the curb. Curbs were a fine new mark of our civilization and therefore an attraction. "Built-in benches for babes" was the way Daddy teased us, but he'd been instrumental in getting them there, so we didn't mind.

We considered curbs our private property and therefore felt perfectly safe sitting there watching the world go by. I sat on the curb to wait for Larona to get home from kindergarten, to watch Brent work on his old Model T, to count cars in a funeral procession, or to watch the couples court by the pine trees on the Capitol grounds. I sat on the curb to float boats in the gutter, so clean in those days with mountain water forever running away. We'd squat to tie a shoe lace or carefully fold down our long lisle stockings on the first warm day of the season.

It was a daily plan for Betty and me to meet halfway at the church on the corner. We sat there for nearly seventeen summers —right on up through high school—surveying the scene or solving the problems of life. The view of the Capitol was perfect. We watched dignitaries come and the wonderfully intricate wrought iron, fencing the state's property, go. We watched people take their driving license tests around the newly created parking lot. Demonstrating parallel parking skill was the tough one for most folks, and we sat shivering in delicious agony about whether we'd pass or not when our turn came—if ever!

You could see all kinds of things from a curb and nobody paid you any mind. It was as if you were part of the scenery. We used to watch Mrs. Widley hang up her wash. Her clothesline was in plain sight of the street. She had much more formal education than other women on the Hill and didn't make a fetish of getting her clothes out first on Monday morning. But she did have a fascinating, undeviating system for setting out the week's laundry when she got around to it.

She hung from the inside lines and worked out. She must have organized everything in the house, because by the time she was finished, the whole thing was shielded by sheets. Mother said the breezes couldn't blow through and fluff things up that way. Every woman had to defend her own habits, I guess. My own opinion was it was too bad to hide all those clothes because they looked so nice the way she did it.

Towels were flipped and folded lengthwise and pinned neatly according to size, color, and use (bathroom, company best, and kitchen), with the washcloths and dishrags separating each kind. Stockings were matched and hung all of a size together in a section of line. Coverall legs were pinned even to the line—three pins per leg—not folded over to leave an ugly bend in the bottom. She'd stretch and pull the cotton T-shirts back into shape and alternate them with the shorts. When they came down, a top and bottom were folded up neatly together. Petticoats and pantywaists were carefully covered with aprons, but the union suits dangled freely from the shoulders to march crazily along the line—dancing in whatever wind—like an army having underwear inspection.

Taking down was done according to a system, too. All the kitchen things were piled together; all the things to be mended and all the starched goods had their stacks. Her work was half done, her ironing greatly lessened with this procedure. We never tired of watching the ritual, and I benefited greatly from such instruction when I became a bride, because it all came back to me the day I did my first wash.

On the Twenty-fourth of July holiday, we'd shift our curb-sitting to the south edge of the Hill. We'd plop down on the curb for a bird's-eye view of the Pioneer Day parade meandering down Main Street. Those wonderfully wide streets Brigham Young had insisted upon allowed all kinds of remarkable band formations and posse performances. And there was plenty of room for a full review.

From where we sat, we could watch the exciting confusion of the gathering and the maneuvering of unwieldy floats between the Hotel Utah and the temple, where the lineup took place. The horses reared under rein, and people crossed and recrossed the street in an endless parade of their own. Nothing stayed put. But then, one by one, the units started past the Brigham Young monument in a miracle of elegant orderliness for public approval and a powerful reminder of their heritage.

I never saw a prettier parade than one back in the twenties when I was a very little girl. Maybe another one has never equaled it, because as I grew older the aura of childhood wonder was outlived by other excitements. But maybe it was because I was in it.

Instead of curb-sitting, this time the family walked on down the Hill together. A close-up seemed important this time. Mom and the others positioned themselves in front of the old Constitution Building. She liked facing the unique store front of Zion's Cooperative Mercantile Institution, and the children could buy refreshment from the heat in the Grabeteria nearby, where Daddy often ate lunch.

I bounced beside Daddy to the Primary Children's Hospital just west of Main across from the north gate of Temple Square. I was to ride on their float. I was in a long white nightgown and had a new ribbon to band over my bangs. My heart was pounding with unfamiliar self-importance. And there it was—the most beautiful of floats awaiting the arrival of its queen. My throne, I soon discovered, was a hospital bed. Well, I could handle that! But what did disturb me was the lady in charge. Fortunately I can't remember who she was, only how she was. I silently figured I never wanted to be "in charge" of anything if that's how it made you be. Her first words when she saw me were, "Good grief! We chose her because she was so skinny she looked sick. Take off that hair ribbon!"

And she yanked it off my head and then began frantically pounding my face with powder—all of my face, eyes, nose, mouth, and even my bangs.

So they chose me because I looked sick! Daddy's tender heart thumped for mine, and when the make-up was finished he asked if I might be taken in to say good-bye to the children in the hospital. Personally I didn't want anybody seeing me like this. If they thought I looked sick before . . .

But Daddy was wisely unwavering. We went in, and the nurse told the children I was to represent them on their float. And then, oh then, what a time it turned out to be! They clapped and they shouted. They thumped their crutches and rocked their wheelchairs.

Hoorah! For *me*!

I was overwhelmed. Humbled. And, oh, mercy, I nearly cried right there in front of everybody. It was only the thought of a repeat on the powdering that helped me hold back the tears.

Then they put me high on the float, in the bed, covered up. My nightgown didn't show. My hair ribbon was gone. My face was an unrecognizable mess. But as we moved out onto Main Street I felt a small surge of usefulness swell deep inside of me as if I had taken all of their terrible suffering onto my skinny shoulders.

And all I had to do was look sick!

All the particulars of past scenes and glad scenes, all the minutiae of delight upon delight, can never equal the joy of that parade.

Unto Others

Summer and winter alike, vacations and holidays notwithstanding, our whole family went to church—everybody, every time. Sometimes it was really interesting, especially when Brother and Sister Rawson performed their duet: he played the harmonica and she whistled. They were genial people who cooked the church suppers or provided entertainment as needed. They each had a huge stomach, and I always wondered how they dared to stand up in public like that with so much of themselves sticking out. But they put on a good act and gave a whole new sound to the hymns. Sometimes Jessie Evans sang "He That Hath Clean Hands" in a way that made me look at mine a second time.

The only way you escaped from the tortures of a boring speaker on a hot summer night was to convince your mother you needed the rest room and couldn't wait until you got home. A speaker knew how well he was doing by the number of children filing out.

One July night we were hearing about the pioneers again, and the speaker was as dry as the plains our ancestors had crossed.

People waved their fans vigorously in a valiant effort to stay awake. I'd already been out, so I was trying to entertain myself by looking at the people. Sometimes that was more fun than anything. Like old Sister Huebner and her fan. Most of us used the cardboard kind passed out to us at the door. There was advertising on the back, like "Is Your Life Insurance Beneficial," with an enormous question mark curling around the slogan. But Mrs. Huebner had a fan made out of cut ivory that collapsed and expanded from a base with a silk tassle dangling. She had a tricky way of using it, too. She'd fan on the downswing, fold up the fan on the upswing, fan on the downswing, fold up on the upswing. About the fifth or sixth sequence her head would begin to nod and she would hit her nose. My brother Lowell and I were betting hairpins from Mother's purse on which stroke she would hit her nose, when suddenly her fan got caught in her nostril! There simply was no stopping our giggles. We stuffed our mouths with handkerchiefs. We hid our red faces in the hymnbook. We suffered Mother to clap her hands over our eyes so we couldn't look at each other and burst out laughing again. But we couldn't stop. It was a marvelous relief to be whisked from the church at last. Disgrace may have been ours for the moment, but so was freedom.

That night, before bed, Mother took us into the dining room to talk to us about Behavior Unto Others. I remember best the part about treating other people as you'd like to be treated, especially when they were trying their best. That's when Heavenly Father smiled upon you, she explained, when you were nice to someone even when you didn't feel like it. Then she kissed us anyway.

One summer Sunday, my friend Vic showed up at our house a while before church and said bread was needed for the sacrament. Mother quickly wrapped two loaves of fresh-from-the-oven bread. Because it was for the sacrament, none of us grumbled much, until later when something very peculiar happened at the meeting. There was a bit of jostling in our aisle by a couple of the deacons, but finally Vic lost the scuffle and had to serve our family the tray of bread bits. Instead of Mother's, it was sticky bakery bread, and as Mother caught his eye Vic went scarlet. After the meeting Mother approached him. Before she could say anything, Vic went through the agonies, protestations, and explanations that guilt generates. When it was her turn to talk, she merely said, "Vic, how would you like to come over and wash my bread pans next time?" Relief, repentance, and the hope of some restitution for the blasphemy of using the sacrament as an excuse for a homemade bread "bust" out in the field, flooded his face. When he finished the job, a day or so later, I noticed Mother gave him two of the crusty ends of new bread.

Summer wasn't going to be ruined after all.

It was our custom to kneel in family prayer. In winter, families were secreted together inside, with sounds of the stoker rattling the coal furnace in the basement and the smell of dinner still fragrant. Prayer didn't seem an interruption then. It was a cozy part of the season. Somebody was always sick, too, and blessings were a valid need.

But in summer, when light still lingered and dogs and children romped in noisy delight on our front lawn, it was different. The voices of the neighborhood kids were a painful distraction, wafting in and out of my consciousness like the furls of a flag in a soft wind, revealing only part of the pattern with each breeze. I'd strain to hear who was already out, what they were saying, which game they were playing while we were still praying. I longed to fly free into the evening cooled by canyon breezes and leave my miserable body there, prostrate over the chair.

We would kneel in the dining room, scene of all formal moments in our family life, each child to a chair so there was less jostling during the prayer. I kept my eyes open until the last moment before the prayer started, studying the hardwood floor marred by an ink spot Junior had made doing his homework, its irregular shape forever on the floor, forever in my mind.

When Daddy prayed, it was always longer. He blessed every-one up and down the block by name. Often I couldn't follow what he said because the words were unfamiliar and the style unlike our comfortable conversations. He'd say things like, "Father, we thank thee that all is in accord and that the personnel of this family is complete and accounted for."

Once I visited his office and heard him dictate letters while I waited for a ride up the hot hill. That was it! His prayers were like he was giving dictation. That night when he prayed, I risked the wrath of heaven and sneaked a look at Daddy's face. I was startled. He was weeping! The language he spoke was formal like his letters to important people, but the tears running down his cheeks spoke volumes about the tenderness in his heart.

Daddy loved Heavenly Father so much that he spoke to him in the best language he knew. It was that experience that made me restless with my habitual bedtime routine "Now I lay me down to sleep. . . ." That summer I ventured a prayer from my heart in my own language instead of reciting something memorized in some-body else's.

Curious Learnings

For years summer began the first Monday after school was out when a fluffy white-haired neighbor lady gathered us girls to help her with the Costumes. We followed her from house to house, Pied-Piper style, panting to keep pace with her. Bits of satin, an old army coat, feathers, and gauzy flowers were collected along with us girls. By getting to us before we were involved in anything else, she was assured of some help from us. But we didn't understand that psychology then. We only knew we were needed for the world's most exciting project — readying costumes in case somebody needed them for the Primary Pageant or the Covered Wagon Day parade.

We threaded elastic and pressed seams. She created costumes, all the while singsonging plans for elaborate productions that might or might not materialize. We were spellbound, but we tired long before she did. When we finally gave out, our Costume General would pass the cookies and then march us all home. Only it wasn't a march. It was more like a dance, because she kept doing a little twirl to encourage the laggers.

There came a summer when I felt too mature for this sort of thing. Mother understood but urged that I go just one more time in an act of appreciation.

"Make her feel your thanks and observe her carefully this time," Mother counseled. "Someday you'll remember that growing old isn't so bad if you stay young."

But staying young didn't seem relevant to me then. I was young. I was immortal. Nothing would ever change.

It did, however, with the appearance in our lives of Blye, who quickly taught me some advantages of growing older. Blye was one of the small-town girls who came to the city to attend summer sessions at the business college at the bottom of the Hill. These girls would find live-in situations with families close by and they'd help around the house in exchange for board and room. Our Blye turned out to be just another member of the family. She shared my room, and I learned from her some curious things about being glamorous. She read movie magazines and tried all of the Secrets of the Stars. I watched her roll her hair on kid curlers with a setting gel she made by cooking flaxseed. I saw her rub Vaseline darkened with a melted brown crayon on her lashes, and she plucked out all of her eyebrows — unheard-of things to do in our neighborhood. She rubbed lemons — precious lemons! — onto her heels and elbows and knuckles. She used K-lotion and glycerine on her hands and Hind's Honey and Almond Cream on her face. She buffed her nails until I thought they would go up in smoke. But the most exciting thing of all was her pink taffeta dress that was shorter in front than in back. The blue satin lining in back framed her legs elegantly and swept to the floor when she walked. She wore it to the stag dances every Saturday night at the Coconut Grove, Salt Lake's answer to Hollywood's seat of excitement. To a girl from the settlement of Santaquin down south, this was something wonderful. To Mother it was a hazard, and she kept a close check.

In the way children have of uncovering things, we discovered that poor Blye couldn't see except up close, and we would ask her the time just so we could watch her squint down with her nose practically on the face of the clock. Then we'd burst into laughter. It happened that Mother got in on one of those disgraceful sessions and shamed us thoroughly. But she learned that Blye needed glasses badly and didn't have the money to get them.

We held a family council later, when Blye was away, and talked about the help she had been to us. Daddy liked the way she giggled at his old jokes and kept his glass filled with water at dinner. Junior said she'd shined his shoes for Sunday School. I was enchanted with the fingerwave (using flaxseed gel!) she'd given me for Beverly's birthday party. Lowell said she wasn't too bad for a girl, and little Nadine clapped for everything. With appreciation and sympathy for her plight and noble unselfishness welling up in our hearts, we decided to finance her trip to the eye doctor. We did it by canceling the family outing to Saltair on the edge of the Great Salt Lake with its enormously exciting giant racer.

I'll never forget the night Dad presented Blye with the finished glasses. She slowly put them on. "What time is it?" we all cried. And Blye looked at the clock from where she sat across the room and told us the time. Then she burst into tears.

Charity beyond the family . . . sisterhood when you had different parents . . . she hadn't complained when we teased nor because she couldn't see . . . how rude we'd been to laugh at her plight . . . how good it felt to make someone happy. These thoughts whirled through my mind as we all sat there silent through her tears. Then I hugged Blye, I was so happy for her, and then everybody hugged everybody else and Mother brought in one of Jell-o's new "six delicious flavors" with whipped cream and sliced bananas for a treat.

A few years later Mother made me my first formal and I chose pink taffeta in honor of Blye. There were two dozen tiny lavender crystal buttons down the back placket, but no zipper. Zippers were new, and Mother hadn't learned how to insert one, so she sewed me into each dress she made for me each time I wore it —

including this pink taffeta. When the doorbell rang she had just finished "sewing me in" and I flew to the door, unrestrained. The porch was empty. Suddenly a tomato hit against the screen door and splattered little black and red specks all over the front of my dress. Then I heard some of the neighborhood boys guffawing as they ran by, taunting me about going out with a boy who lived off the Hill. In their tracks appeared my date, and my heart sank. It was my only formal. There wasn't time to get unsewn, cleaned, resewn. I was standing where he could see me, anyway.

"The options are clear," Mother said matter-of-factly. "You can stay home in false pride and ruin a nice evening or forget yourself and smile a lot. No one will notice the spots then."

So I smiled. I even smiled when I saw those jokesters at church the next day.

But that summer I mastered the sewing skill of inserting a zipper.

A Little
Out of the Sun

Summer rain was precious in our desert valley. Even a mid-August mist was cause for a celebration. It was the great common denominator, too. People would stand on their porches in a down-pour smiling broadly and waving across the torrents tirelessly. Rain was vital for the crops, for our cool — and for us kids it determined whether the clay cave could be played in.

The first thing we did in a rainstorm was eagle claws with a ball bat. The one whose hand grasp reached the lip on the bat handle last was declared official judge of the clay's readiness. We used that system for solving all kinds of important arguments, like who had to wash the dishes instead of wipe, who got to post the flag on the porch pillar for the Fourth, and who sat next to Grandma at Sunday dinner. (This latter was a dubious privilege, because she'd make us clean our plates till they looked "slicked licked," and yet we could quietly examine the holes in her ears, where her jewelry hung, until our curiosity was thoroughly satiated.)

Well, when the "heavens opened good and proper," as Mr. Korth used to say, pontificating after the fact, we'd wait a couple of hours and then start haunting the small cave on the side of the hill off Wall Street. We'd scoop up a handful of earth and mash it between our fingers, debating its readiness. Ground rules were that we could give an opinion but we had to wait for an official decision from our "judge." Timing was so critical. When the rain seepage had reached the clay bed, you just had to be on hand. Too long a wait meant the clay would crumble. Too soon and the stuff wasn't moist enough. After a summer storm you just had to stall chores and forgo outings if you cared about clay. I cared about clay.

I got so I could pretty well tell when it was going to rain. First I'd watch for a yellow sunset. A yellow sunset was more than a fisherman's warning, it was an absolutely summer novelty over our Great Salt Lake where the sun went down like thunder in the summer and the skies were fired past bedtime. A yellow sunset was sign of a storm, and the sulphur smells would rise from the lake. Next I'd check Woolley's poplar trees for verification. When the white side of the leaves showed, we'd get out the umbrellas for the morrow.

I remember one time when the storm was so spectacular the dried June grass couldn't hold the soil, and rivulets wrinkled the hill. The neighbors talked of a mud flood, and the Capitol flower beds had to be built up all over again. But the quality of the clay in the cave was never better. Why, it was like I had magic in my hands, and the fever of creation raced my pulse. I was oblivious to present company as I squeezed, pinched, and patted my own reasonable facsimile of Massasoit, who at that time graced the Capitol rotunda. This heroic-size bronze statue was our introduction to sculpture and heightened our reverence for the integrity of the American Indian. Massasoit was the Indian chief who first greeted the Pilgrims. The fact that Cyrus Dallin, a native Utahn, had created this monument for faraway Plymouth Rock was impressive to me. So, sheltered though we were, the near nudity of this massive statue never embarrassed us, much less fascinated us unduly.

But it greatly disturbed one of the old maids who lived nearby to see me sculpting a naked man when she crossed the street to give the message that I was wanted for dinner. She was an important church worker and made sure we said our prayers when we slept over with her niece. And of course, since she didn't play around the Capitol, how could she know a Massasoit when she saw one? She made such a fuss about the "goings on" in that cave with "innocent children" that it was declared out-of-bounds by all the parents.

Mother's pride was fierce, and she couldn't bear the thought that her "lovely little daughter" had been misjudged, she was sure! You see, when I explained to Mother about Massasoit, she walked me right back to the cave to hunt for the sculpture that had been dropped during the trauma of a "lady apostle's" (as we called her behind her back) lecture on virtue. Mother wanted to see my work for herself.

We found Massasoit all right, miraculously all of a piece though somewhat misshapen. Mother handled it very carefully, smoothing the cold, damp surface of the unfinished, innocent work. She turned it around and around thoughtfully. Her smile was kind. Her eyes even lit up some but then saddened.

"Look, Elaine, this is very nicely done. Why don't you hurry up and make a feather for his headband and get a loincloth in place. Then we'll walk over to Sister Beesley's home to show her what you really had in mind. You might even want to scratch your signature in the clay and make her a present of it."

She didn't want the sculpture, but Mother was satisfied that the dear sister understood my intentions.

Needless to say, I did not grow up to become a native Utah sculptor with my work in far places. Anyway, for me it was more important that I come to an understanding of viewpoint. Perspective. In his *Pieta*, Michelangelo portrayed Christ dead. Thorvaldsen, in his *Christus*, saw him living. And being positive was better than being negative, Mother explained, as we studied pictures of the beautiful works of the master sculptors.

But I didn't go back to the cave again, and seldom did a summer have so many good rains.

There was another side to summer storms, and that was what they did to sandbox castles and playhouses.

For a proper playhouse, we'd take all day to drape blankets, old curtains, and burlap bags the canning sugar came in. We'd swag them from fruit tree to fruit tree, to the clothesline pole and back again, with room after room being bounded by the beginnings and endings of blankets and burlap. By the time we'd finish the hang-and-tie treatment it was day's end, and I'd usually check the sunset so I could try to pray away the yellow if it showed in the west.

One day we had put up a particularly elaborate affair, with plans to hold our club meetings there until the weekend, when it would have to come down so the lawn could be cut. We even designated a portion of it as a tent to hide the boys' rubber guns. This way they wouldn't pester our plans and Daddy couldn't confiscate the guns, which had been declared dangerous weapons. The rubber gun was notched out of a wooden crate with a newfangled spring clothes pin nailed at the trigger end. The boys cut narrow strips of old inner tube, which were stretched from the gun point and secured in the clothes pin. When you pinched the pin, it released the rubber. That ammunition could sting if you were a target and it hit its mark! Naturally this ingenious item did not win a parental seal of approval, so the playhouse was a great new cache.

The dawn after these labors, I think I smelled the rain before I heard it, and I tightened my eyes firmly against waking to the reality of ruin in our backyard. I lay there for long minutes considering what to do. I could bury my face in my pillow and sleep out the storm, or I could get up and watch the destruction take place. I got up.

I remember standing there mentally reciting in rhythm with the rain, "On a misty, moisty morning when cloudy was the weather . . ." I said that nursery rhyme over and over pointlessly. I kept wishing some old man in leather would come along to save the sog from happening to our blankets sopping it up out there.

Instead my older brother appeared sleepily by my side. "It's a mess, isn't it?"

Why did he have to say it out loud like that? Once labeled, that's also what I saw it as. It was indeed a miserable mess that we would have to clean up. Of course I began to cry.

"Oh, what are you kicking about?" he asked flatly. "Half the fun was getting it up."

Well, you don't forget insight like that!

That same brother talked me through many a storm in life, and as the years passed he emerged as my hero, my knight, my prince charming, my dreamboat. Very early I resigned myself to the second-citizen class for husband material because I figured there simply wasn't anybody else that smart around.

Or good-looking.

When he graduated from high school, I followed him every place he'd let me while he got ready. High school seniors in those days didn't have caps and gowns for commencement. They cost money to rent. And who had money like that? Graduation was usually the time a boy acquired his first suit. Or he borrowed one.

Junior's was a brown blazer with white flannel slacks that he wore with argyle socks and saddle shoes. We'd all sacrificed some for that outfit, but it was worth it. He was splendid. I gazed fondly, chin in hand, while he tied and retied his tie, then combed and recombed his hair so it would slick straight back from his brow. Then he posed for a Kodak shot, trying hard not to smile.

"Stand a little out of my sun," he said grandly, giving me a gentle jab in the ribs. Then he rewarded my worship by adding, "and thanks, in advance, beautiful, for not telling anyone I put Vaseline on my hair."

Beautiful! Me? To him? Oh, what an absolutely marvelous night! Why, I'd stand a little out of the sun, walk through the rain, anything at all—except clean out the garbage closet—for that brother!

The Summer
of My Content

There was the summer of love just before "our" war. The serious rumblings that echoed across oceans were crowded from my heart by one older boy. I operated at fever level with a sweeping love for life, friends, and my family, for tennis, for twilight and the morning skies, for poetry, and for Glenn Miller himself, whose music accompanied almost every move I made. I painted my nails to "String of Pearls" and beat fudge to the rhythm of "Little Brown Jug." But "Sunrise Serenade" was "our" song, and I'd play it over and over again while I'd record the details of my life in a five-year diary which had a lock and key.

His name filled the pages. There was summer in his voice, and every word he uttered in my presence, the way his hair swirled from the crown of his head, his strong jawline and one injured thumbnail, all found place in my diary. Clippings of his basketball games were stuffed in the back. If he laughed at something somebody said, I laughed too. Only I wished I'd said such a clever thing so he'd find pleasure in me. If he shifted to tenor in the campfire sing-along, I'd shift to alto for closer harmony. I said his name like a prayer when I fell off to sleep, and I practiced writing it with "Mrs." in front of it, sometimes with a fancy flourish, sometimes with a cool, sophisticated slant.

All of this emotional involvement on my part while he went on tossing the *Deseret News* on the porches of the Hill without a pause before our door.

One night at a church dance a miracle occurred. He asked me to dance. My moment had arrived, and all the articles I'd read on charm were now to be applied. I would impress him. He would never forget me. What actually happened was that I began chattering to reveal to him my clever wit and brilliance, my darling personality.

Very shortly he stopped dancing, moved away from me though still holding me in his arms, and said, with the patience and wisdom of Age, "Elaine, one doesn't talk during 'Stardust.' "

One doesn't talk during "Stardust"! All the passion of my heart rushed to my throat and lodged there. I resolved then and there to dedicate my life to helping girls understand what really worked with boys. Obviously my own authorities had been wrong.

There came a time shortly after that when I talked about love to Daddy, whose eyes crinkled with tender tears and whose voice sounded funny when we children made him the most pitiful present, when we performed at school, or when he introduced us to his friends.

"To love is to live," he explained. "To be loved in return is God's gift. Think about loving, Elaine, not being loved. One day the richest kind of gift will be yours."

Oh, Daddy knew about loving.

"Upon those who love, ungenerous time bestows a thousand summers," someone once said. How true that is for me! Sunrise after sunrise over the Wasatch Range. Sunset blending with sunset behind the Oquirrhs and turning that copper Capitol dome into a fiery thing. So many summers that the counting is a chore, but with memories enough to have been a thousand.

As summers came and went, each brought its own reward, each requiring something of me. My own marriage pressed young upon me because of war. Then, yet another baby to nurse, another batch of fruit to preserve, another church assignment to fill, another marriage of a beloved child. Until at last, there came one summer's end, a gathering of our family one last time before the youngest would leave for his mission.

We were at the cabin, a little place we had built ourselves in great sacrifice and joy, sharing efforts and sore thumbs with the wonderful larger family of grandparents, uncles, aunts, and cousins as close now as siblings.

We treasured this primitive place where so many summers had been spent so close to stars and wild creatures of the earth and away from the stores and shocks of civilization.

I looked at these I loved and would give my life for — grown-ups themselves now — circling the fire and quietly considering the question their father had put to us, "Well, what have you learned this summer?"

The one preparing for a mission spoke first. "My work at the restaurant put me in company with some people with a life-style far different from ours. It's been quite an eye-opener. But then I began noticing how they behaved with rude customers so free with complaints and insults. I learned that 'the soft answer turneth away wrath.'"

The young wife spoke almost with reverence. "I have learned about love. Bryant loves me anyway. And such love makes me want to please him. I'm beginning to understand something about Heavenly Father's ability to love us even when we aren't doing our best."

There had been a recent funeral for a friend of one of our girls, and she had been deeply touched by the fine things said about him at the service. "I thought at the time," she said quietly, "what would they be able to say at my funeral — that I was a good dresser? Bob's death is a dramatic thrust for me to live with more purpose. That's what I've learned this summer."

And so it went, each reporting on books read and discoveries made, of skills sharpened and friendships strengthened, of scriptures memorized and principles reaffirmed, and of the wonder of bearing a child.

"How could the mother of Jesus stand to lose him?" whispered the young mother hugging her firstborn.

It was the summer of my content.

In spite of financial reverses, threatening changes, critical illness, pressures of responsibilities, lost youth, and tender nostalgia, I felt the spilling of my cup as I sat in the circle of my family. This is what living is all about.

My world had broadened beyond the Hill, but my heart still found solace in the lessons of those years. Coping is contagious.

From oleander to grandmother, with my life now matching the season, I am akin to Albert Camus. "In the midst of winter I finally learned that there was in me an invincible summer."